About the Author

The author has studied English and American Literature and works as an English teacher. She has also worked as a radio producer, DJ and lyricist. Her infinite love though has always been poetry and it's the only way she finds comfortable enough to communicate. This book is a dive into the author's life and experiences without filters or sugar-coating.

"I hope you will enjoy reading it and maybe, be able to relate a little. I hope it will make you feel that you are not alone."

J K

Melina Amalia Vavoula

J K

Olympia Publishers
London

www.olympiapublishers.com
OLYMPIA PAPERBACK EDITION

Copyright © Melina Amalia Vavoula 2023
Cover by Maximos Manolis

The right of Melina Amalia Vavoula to be identified as author of this work has been asserted in accordance with sections 77 and 78 of the Copyright, Designs and Patents Act 1988.

All Rights Reserved

No reproduction, copy or transmission of this publication may be made without written permission.
No paragraph of this publication may be reproduced, copied or transmitted save with the written permission of the publisher, or in accordance with the provisions
of the Copyright Act 1956 (as amended).

Any person who commits any unauthorised act in relation to this publication may be liable to criminal prosecution and civil claims for damage.

A CIP catalogue record for this title is available from the British Library.

ISBN: 978-1-80439-286-7

This is a work of fiction.
Names, characters, places and incidents originate from the writer's imagination. Any resemblance to actual persons, living or dead, is purely coincidental.

First Published in 2023

Olympia Publishers
Tallis House
2 Tallis Street
London
EC4Y 0AB

Printed in Great Britain

Dedication

This book is dedicated to my beloved daddy, Konstantinos Vavoulas, that I tremendously miss and my mum, Denise.

Acknowledgements

I want to thank all my close friends that kept me going through the years and all the people that gave me feelings inspiring enough to write about. A special thanks to my friend journalist Sotiris Karamintzas.

01.

Hurricane I

My mind is like a hurricane, full of beautiful and yet awful things
a labyrinth where every thought gets lost and dies by brightly burning into ash.
I love seeing them burn, embraced by fire's deadly arms;
a sight so magnetising that deprives of breath the ones able to see it
so every night, as I go to bed, I dream of fire.

02.

Truth

Human instincts are always near
and they always lead to tears.
Hearts get broken, souls left open,
floating in a sea of pity and disgrace.
We'll all drown in our shame,
through our pain,
we are led to absolution and the truth.

03.

True Love

LOVE is not to be afraid.
LOVE is not to be afraid, to bury a part of you, for someone else's integrity.
LOVE is not to be afraid, to manifest your truth, your rawest sentiment, your pain and insecurities, your lust or even your anger.
LOVE is the ability to put yourself on display in its purest instinctual form,
with no repression, no unnecessary words, completely uninhibited.
An epiphany.

04.

Hurricane II

I dream of fire and blood
then wake up soaked by the rain;
a rush so eager, a hush consuming the letters of all the words
that will remain unspoken and unwritten, forbidden,
withdrawn lost in the unknown.
You'll make fire turn to ice; a stiff feeling I so despise.

05.

With You

When I'm with you, I don't know what to say or do.
I lose the sense of space and time lingering in a sky divine.
Denying all that once was mine, what kept me going all my life.
My tough 'n' solid steel walls, you've smashed them down, seen my soul.
A soul so bare, afraid to share, used only to stand and stare, now just wants to be devoured by your corrupted mouth.
So drug me down, bless me with sin and glorify the lust within.

06.

Blind

Now I stand here waiting, anticipating and aching,
I can hear my own heart breaking and in the molecules of time,
lingers your smell that's still divine.
By thee, my being has been defined, raw power that shaped my life.
Stripped me off from all my pride and all the ethereal light, leaving me motionless and blind in the darkness some call life.

07.

The Face

Missing your face, the air full of your trace,
your tormented grace has me consumed,
A feeling doomed, a crave never-ending,
selfish, destructive yet tempting.

08.

Infinite and Incomplete

The silver moon shines bright in the sky,
spreading light in the black void of the night,
tenderly empty and sharp it cuts the skin;
you breathe it in,
infinite but incomplete.

09.

Constant Fight

Wasting my youth, screaming my truth, crawling my way upwards,
I'm in hell's bottom where all is blank, the inner self has me imprisoned
for all these years facing your treason, a thrust so constant
killing me and bringing me back to life,
a fight for light, a chance to thrive.

10.

Encore

Lost in the night,
tormented by the morning light,
indulged in lust, entombed by the past,
awaiting to be free at last.
Your kiss of fire burnt me to the core,
but still came back for an encore.

11.

The Pulse

Desire and fire entwined before my eyes
he was, the pulse of my heart.
Walking around covered in scars,
battles he lost, his will he tossed,
a wandering hole, the blackest of all.
Fading and glowing at the same time
right there before my eyes.

12.

The Dust That Didn't Last

Days go by, words run dry
a world expired
filled with desire
consume me like fire
turn me into dust, my love
I knew it could never last
the entire world will pass us by,
our thoughts will face demise
but still my soul will be melting in your eyes.

13.

Your Reflection

There are times when the abyss in my head stares back at me,
making my heart stop for a while,
and there I find you again.

14.

Hungry Heart

Confused, abused, douched in booze,
playing it all to win or lose,
deceived, conceived, kind of relieved
wounded but strong
I have moved on
and then again falling apart
giving it all for my hungry heart.

15.

Cure Me

You are the cure to my eternal sadness,
allow me to worship your madness,
thus, in darkness we shall thrive,
feeding our demons with life.

16.

Annihilation

For all the times I've been the ice,
chilling your little heart with lies,
for all I've done that's been denied,
always keeping me deprived
of my own vigorous fire,
to thy all that did backfire.

17.

Presence

My spirit lingers in the air and you're only left to stare always knowing that you care even when you're not there.

18.

Stellar Gaze

The times we danced and dreamt,
dazzled by the music of the night.
The power of your gaze piercing through my brain.
Your energy reflecting on me.
All the stellar substance you are made of,
cannot be erased, nor tamed,
compared, overcome or found in any other.
The unconditional, uncontrollable urge,
To live, to breathe, to contain you…
But never to constraint you.

19.

Swallow Me Whole

We live like vampires only under the black sky
our eyes burnt by the morning sun
a hole in my soul that's swallowing me whole
feeling so small
may your darkness be our guide
let's get lost into the night
making the sky shine bright
staring at each other's eyes.

20.

You Are the Sea

Your eyes have me drawn like the sea
your smile makes the sun look dim
your luminous soul tempts my entire being
there's nothing to be compared to thee
through your sight, a new world I'm able to see.

21.

Sweet Disaster

You make my heart beat faster,
you little sweet disaster
running in wilderness and rage
always drowning in vain
by my power and grace.

22.

The Eternal Rider

Riding he came with eyes like coal fire
filled my heart with desire
setting my soul on fire
and just with one eternal kiss
brought me back from the abyss.

23.

Worlds' Collision

There he stood all made of scars
both soul and flesh ones
abusing power given by desire
with a gaze of pure wildfire
shining like a polar light
in the darkness he was embarrassed by
waiting for his world to collide with mine.

24.

Acid Down My Throat

To you, I'm transparent; a girl you look at but never see.
The constant giver
your number-one believer
you cunning deceiver
soul violator
the biggest traitor
pouring acid down my throat
poison
poison
death you are
concealed by the mask of love
destroyed and torn
beyond human control
a carcass you drained
for your own vain
such a disgrace!

25.

J K

I breathe the air, it ain't enough
I see the sky's blue faded
the wind can no longer touch my skin
and thus, vacant I shall wander
in search of thunder
you took the sparkle
removed the light
leaving me stained
for all my life
cursed the knowledge you supplied
the difference of existence to LIFE.